PARLIAMO GLASGOW

PARLIAMO GLASGOW

Stanley Baxter

with

Alex Mitchell

Paul Harris Publishing

Edinburgh

First published 1982 by
Paul Harris Publishing
40 York Place
Edinburgh

ISBN 0 86228 055 9

Printed in Scotland by John G. Eccles Printers Ltd., Inverness

CONTENTS

Illustrated with the many faces of Stanley Baxter

Preface

For thirty-two years I have shared with Alex Mitchell an obsession with the English language as spoken by various sections of Glasgow's population. Long and earnest study of the subject enabled us to become tri-lingual.

Apart from speaking our own basic Scots, we were, after a time, able to speak with and understand the unusual and interesting pronunciation adopted by many maidens and matrons who inhabit what estate agents are wont to describe as "select residential districts" of the city.

The uvular "r" employed by these suburban ladies results from putting the tip of the tongue far back in the roof of the mouth. The "r" sound thus achieved is quite different from the trilling "r" favoured by Sir Harry Lauder and others of the brrraw brrricht munelicht nicht genre anxious to establish to the world their trrrue Scottishness.

The suburban uvular "r" in conjunction with flattened vowels produces such variants of English pronunciation as "Jainnefer end Ai waint to Maureen's coffeh mawrning" and "Ai hed to bai a wee het fawr Sementha's waidding." I have enjoyed trying to portray these genteel ladies on stage and television.

As the melodramatic hero of an early film melodrama.

Other Glaswegians have their own distinctive patois. They show a sturdy Scottish defiance of standard English pronunciation, replacing the "th" sound with "r", glottally-stopping "t" and giving each vowel a unique poetic resonance.

The late great Glasgow comedian, Tommy Morgan, a master of what he termed "the Glesca pattur", first made us aware of this delightful language. He told us how he saw a young native of the city pointing out to a friend two comely damsels whose acquaintance they seemed eager to make. "Errurrowrerr", he announced — in ordinary English, "There they are, over there."

The beauty of the word "Errurrowrerr" appealed to Alex and me. We discussed how an eminent philologist might research into and lecture on a language enriched by this and other picturesque words, such as "Haunus-rapoorie" ("Hand me the milk jug"), "Amferbilin" ("I am extremely warm") and "Whorzyurwallizwulli?" ("Where are your dentures, William?").

And so was born my Professor character, an enthusiastic but rather naive savant who gives learned disquisitions on the habits and language of certain Glasgow citizens.

One might have thought that this incursion into Glaswegian semantics was enough for us. Not so. Some twenty years ago fellow-student Mitchell was watching the B.B.C.'s television Italian lesson, Parliamo Italiano, and he wondered what viewers might make of a similar programme designed to teach them the Glasgow language. Thereupon the first version of that piece of linguistic fantasy, Parliamo Glasgow, was concocted.

Aiding and abetting me in perpetrating Parliamo Glasgow have been, at various times, those gifted Scottish players Doris McLatchie, Una McLean, Hannah Gordon, John Grieve and Angus Lennie. I am grateful to them and to a succession of clever lovelies, the dancers in various pantomimes who have helped me to bring to the attention of the public the intriguing intricacies of a language which, I hope, will never die.

Stanley Baxter

Parliamo Glasgow

At the Discotheque

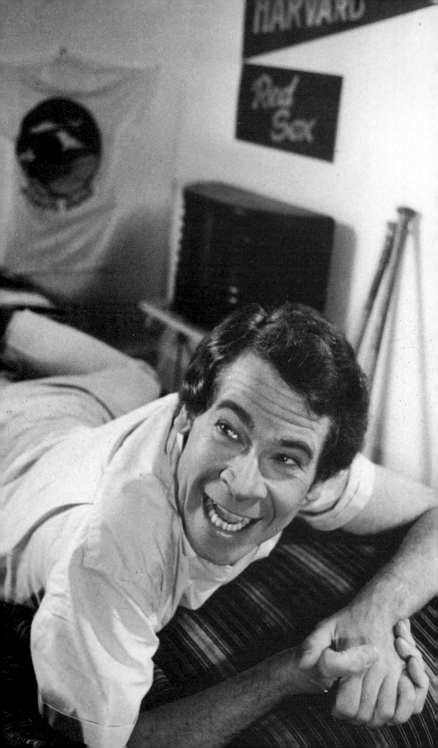

LECTURER: In certain discotheques in Glasgow the more obscure words and phrases used by the native dancers may not be understood by non-Glasgwegian patrons. As one enters such an establishment one may hear the word —
MASHUR
This can form a greeting when the letter "O" is put in front of it and added to it is the word —
SELSOTIZ
And there is our greeting —
OMASHURSELSOTIZ
In English — "Oh my, it is yourself, so it is". Again —
MASHUR
is often employed by a young man in a disco when he first catches sight of a prepossessing damsel. This time, however, it is preceded by three words —
AWANNI

The hospital student in a Broadway medical musical dreams of a career in showbiz.

GERRAHODDA and
RATS
and so we have the fervent declaration
—

AWANNI GERRAHODDA RATS MASHUR
He thus indicates that he wishes to take hold of the young lady and dance with her . . .
Of course, the word undergoes a subtle change of meaning when used by a gentleman who finds dancing a rather warm proceeding. He will then exclaim
—

MASHUR
This is quickly followed by the words —
TAIL
STIKKINTI
MABAHOOKI
which gives us the dramatic disclosure
—

MASHURTAIL STIKKINTIMABAHOOKI
Another interesting word heard in the discotheque is
JIWANNI
To a young lady a gentleman will make the request —
JIWANNI DANCE?
Should she find that he is over-anxious to ply her with refreshments she will regard him with suspicion and inquire —
JIWANNI GETMIBEVVID?

JIWANNI

in certain circumstances changes to —

JIWANNA

used generally in conjunction with the word —

BELTOANRAMOOTH

A female dancer who is sneered at by another maiden may threaten her detractor with facial damage. And so she utters the sinister sentence —

JIWANNABELTOANRAMOOTH?

When a young lady is invited to a gentleman's flat for "coffee or something" she knows intuitively what the "something" is. Thereupon she will reply in ringing tones —

KAMMACOO

It is part of the traditional answer many Glaswegian damsels give to dubious nocturnal invitations and is invariably preceded by —

JIHING

Her full reply to the gentleman's proposition is —

JIHINGKAMMACOO?

I chanced to hear a young lady give such a reply to a forward fellow from outwith the city. He said "I don't get it." Quick as a flash his fair companion assured him —

BIGOADANYEDONTMAC!

The Professor on
A Glaswegian Summer Holiday

One of my most vivid memories of Glasgow is that of the lovely old city's celebrated jour de fete or, to give it its Keltic designation, the Day of Fair Setter, or Fair Setter Day.

As I hastened into the street to join in the revelry I found the air filled with the traditional festival song — "ERRARAINOANU . . . SCUMMINDOONINBUCK-ITS!" I was advised to follow the merry throng leaving the metropolis to take train and steamship to the carnival city of Rothesay. But first, how was I to proceed thereto?

I requested directions of a sturdy young native who was resting at a street corner. Alas the youth did not appear to be versed in the English language. His only answer to my query was a lilting Gaelic phrase signifying his regret at being unable to assist me. "AWORRAL", he sighed, "AWORRALKNOACK-YURHEIDAFF".

Fortunately a small patriarchal gentleman perceived our linguistic impasse and came to my assistance. "CENTRUL STATION," he intoned. Then, to my amazement, he commenced to conjugate one of the

Portraying a nervous little man facing up to Magnus in the Baxter version of 'Mastermind'.

lesser-known Latin verbs — "GERRABUS . . . NORIS-BUS . . . ANURRABUS . . . O, HEERABUS!" I complimented him on his erudition and hired a taxicab to convey me to the Central Station.

As I entered the imposing old edifice the very spirit of Mardi Gras was abroad. Still the glad cries came from the ecstatic vacationers. A large matron gave voice to what sounded to me like the rallying cry of a Highland clan — "IZFURGOATRABLIDDITICKITS!" Soon I was being carried on a wave of happy humanity towards the train.

I was not sorry to find a corner seat and I put my bowler hat down beside me. Judge of my surprise when I was addressed by two young ladies who were obviously of Burmese descent. One damsel declared, "ERRA-SATE." Her companion quickly riposted with "WHERRASATE?" Then the first young lady regarded me with a quizzical air and uttered a strange-sounding Eastern phrase — "ZATSATETOOK?" I could only shake my head. Suddenly, to my astonishment, the stouter of the two maidens sat down upon my hat . . . However, she apologised with yet another pretty Burmese phrase — "FLYMANU SATESTOOKNOO."

At Wemyss Bay as we formed a queue for embarkation in the ship for Rothesay the word "TAKYUR!" came frequently to my ears. "TAKYURTIME!" urged a gentleman heavily burdened with luggage; "TAKYURBA-GAFFMAFIT!" called a lady; and a comely maiden observed to a gallant near her . . . TAKYURHONNAFF-MABUM!"

It was not long ere the ship arrived at the island paradise of Rothesay. As I walked along the promenade

I was astonished by the cosmopolitan aspect of the visitors. On all sides gentlemen of the Mohammedan persuasion were calling out "ALLAH! ALLAH! . . . ALLA-HAWAFURRAPINT", . . . "ALLAHAWAFURRAHAUF" and "ALLAHAWANGITSTOCIOUS".

Later, in a hostelry, I was in conversation with one of these gentlemen and he told me the names of some of his fellow-travellers. I was astounded to learn that they were undoubtedly of Chinese ancestry. "See," said my new-found friend, "He is HAUF FU . . . He is JISTA-BOOT FU and he is BUNG FU." A gentleman who had seated himself on the floor was designated FU AZZA-WULK. I made bold to question Mr Fu Azzawulk as to his place of origin in Ancient China. He looked up at me and answered in the language of his forefathers — "ALHINGWAN OANYU."

I learned much during my sojourn amongst the Glaswegian natives on the glamorous island of Bute. I append a glossary of some of the more obscure words in their fascinating language.

SOFFIKOLRADAY

Today's temperature is extremely low.

SLIKRADEIDAWINTER

The temperature is reminiscent of that experienced in December.

MASPUDZIZLOUPIN

The typical summer weather has reactivated my chilblains.

RATWINZAPEST

That wind is a nuisance.

BELLAZBROLLIZBLEWOOT

Bella's umbrella has been rendered useless by the gale.

RAINZOANAGAIN
The weather is back to normal.
SJISTASHOOR
I am making an optimistic weather forecast.
SAFNU!
The downpour has ceased.
RASUNZOOT
A miracle has taken place!

Parliamo Glasgow

The Engagement Party

LECTURER:	This lecture on Glasgwegianology commences with a playlet about a young lady and her sweetheart who are attending a party to celebrate the engagement of their friend Nancy. As they stand together in a corner surveying the guests they converse in their native tongue . . .
GIRL:	It wiz nice O' Nancy invitin' us yins tae hur pairty.
YOUNG MAN:	Aye.
GIRL:	Therr's Nancy's financy, Wee Clancy . . . a right chancer.
YOUNG MAN:	Hoo can Nancy fancy rat chancer Clancy fur a financy?
GIRL:	He's in ra money.
YOUNG MAN:	She's in ra club.
GIRL:	Haud yur bliddy tongue! A FEMALE IN THE BACKGROUND STARTS TO SING "VOLARE" Whissat noise?
YOUNG MAN:	It's Carrie Balharrie singin' "Volare".

Horror depicted by cockney char on discovering the body of her murdered employer.

GIRL:	Carrie Balharrie fancies Harry Barrie. They're gaun' ragither.
YOUNG MAN:	Aw rat singin's hellish! So depressin' . . . Ah waant anurra hauf.
GIRL:	So dae Ah.
YOUNG MAN:	(CRANING TO LOOK AT BOTTLES ON TABLE) The booze huz ran oot! Jist sody watter left! Let's go!
GIRL:	We canny leave yit! We're no' long here.
YOUNG MAN:	C'm oan doon tae ra pub. Ra baur's no' faur.
GIRL:	Lissen, sodyheid, Ah'm no' leavin' . . . Ah'm jist thinkin'.
YOUNG MAN:	That's a nuvvulty.
GIRL:	Carrie Balharrie's dancin' wi' Harry Barrie but she's winkin' tae Gary Parry.
YOUNG MAN:	Look, Ah'm gaun' oot fur a hauf. You can stey an' puzzle oot the question.
GIRL:	Whit question?
YOUNG MAN:	Wull Carrie Balharrie marry Harry Barrie or Gary Parry?

*　　　*　　　*　　　*

LECTURER:	The conversation of the young lady and her sweetheart, or lumbur, at Nancy's engagement party provides us with some interesting words and phrases. Let us examine a few of these.

It seems obvious that neither is in favour of Nancy's betrothal to the diminutive Mr Clancy. At once the young man uses the word —
HOOKIN
To this he appends a more striking word and this gives us —
HOOKINNANCIFANCIRATCH-
ANCERCLANCIFURRAFINANCY?
The young lady explains the eligibility of Mr Clancy by employing what would appear to be a Persian expression —
IZZINRAMUNNI
Her escort thereupon surveys the contours of the newly-engaged maiden and announces his verdict with another Middle Eastern term —
SHEEZZINRA
Under the impression that Nancy has become a member of some organisation, he states firmly —
SHEEZZINRACLUB
His fair companion refutes the allegation that her friend is too involved in club activities and exclaims —
HODJUR
using it in conjunction with a German noun —
BLIDDITUNG
thus making the emphatic request —
HODJURBLIDDITUNG
HODJUR, of course, is used in other

contexts. A lady who finds that her husband is incapacitated after partaking of refreshments may add to it a word derived from the Japanese language —

KINYINO

as she make the inquiry —

KINYINOHODJURBEVVI?

HODJUR is sometimes prefixed by the syllable "AL" and it becomes —

ALHODJUR

A lady seeking to chastise another lady may avail herself of a friend's offer —

ALHODJURHONBAG

This in turn precedes another word borrowed from an obscure Indian dialect —

TIYUBASHUR

So the offer made to the aggressive lady reads —

ALHODJURHONBAGTIYUBASHUR

But let us return to the words used by the young couple at the engagement party. The young man explains to his inamorata that a female guest is rendering an Italian ballad —

CARRIBALHARRISINGINVOLARE

The damsel then discloses that Miss Balharrie has formed a romantic attachment to a Mr Barrie —

CARRIBALHARRIFANCISHARRI-

BARRI

She signifies that their association is a close one, using the expressive native phrase —

RURGON RUGIRRUR

But her escort, the lumbur, is not interested in the details of Miss Balharrie's courtship. He has made the disconcerting discovery that the supply of alcoholic beverages at the party has become exhausted. He urges the young lady to accompany him to licensed premises. In a telling sentence he reveals —

RABORZNOFAUR

But his comely companion refuses to leave the function and is lost in thought, wondering why Miss Carrie Balharrie, while dancing with Mr Harry Barrie, is winking to another gentleman, a Mr Gary Parry. Her own lumbur, still anxious to visit the nearby hostelry, suggests that she should puzzle out the question for herself. "Whit question?" she inquires. In a word of the most enchanting poesy the young man enlightens her —

WULCARRIBALHARRIMARRIHAR-RIBARRIORGARRIPARRI?

The Professor on
Hogmanay

How exhilarating it was to sojourn once more in Glasgow, that charming citadel of tradition and culture. By a happy chance my arrival coincided with the ancient and picturesque Festival of Hogmanay or, as it is known in the native patois, RA BIG BOOZE-UP.

It was my good fortune to meet with a gentleman who invited me to accompany him to the sacred Hogmaniacal rites at a residence in the remote Southern terrain of the city called RASOOSIDE.

When I suggested that it might be expedient to engage a taxicab my companion mentioned a lady's name. "NORAH!" he said, "NORAHBLIDDICHANCE." Before I could question him as to the lady's identity he made certain obscure references to snow and the Yukon . . . "SNOWFAUR", he stated, "YUKONHOOFIT".

Alas, the gentleman and I began to find that our safari was somewhat fatiguing. Happily we were able to take our ease in each of the seven taverns we discovered along our route. When we entered the last of these delightful havens of rest we encountered a truly festive scene. There was a merry ringing of bells and those who

Aged by a decade or three to appear as that great comedian, George Burns.

dispensed the refreshments were wishing their patrons well with heartfelt cries of "RABELLZWENT!" "SEFTURTIME!" and "BAURZSHUT!" A gentleman who was favouring the company with a song was courteously thanked with the old Doric word, "YUVHUDDANUFFMAC".

As we reached the residence that was to be the scene of the ceremonies I was full of the spirit of the old Caledonian Hogmanay Festival. What a gracious Scottish reception was accorded me by the other participants! They gathered round me and bade me welcome with the age-old Gaelic salutation — "HUZZIBRUNGA!" "HUZZIBRUNGA!" . . . "HUZZIBRUNG-ACERRYOOT?" When I presented my hostess with a modest package of wine-gums she thanked me in the lilting language of her Hebridean forefathers. "MEANJIOL!" she murmured, "MEANJIOLBAMPOAT!"

A little later I became aware of the fact that two damsels near me were discussing the hostess. From their conversation I deduced that the lady had been engaged in a romance with a lover from some tropical clime. "She has," declared one of the damsels, "a black bun in the oven."

But it did my heart good to observe how enthusiastically those simple natives entered into the spirit of the proceedings. I noticed one stout patriarch performing a lively ceremonial dance on top of a coffee table. The onlookers signified their appreciation with ecstatic calls of "GERRIM!" . . . "GERRIMAFFRATABLE!" "GERRIM OOTAHERE!" and "GERRIMTAEHISSCRATCHUR!"

The carnival was continuing with a gaiety that was

contagious when, suddenly, a regrettable mishap occurred. A plump lady who had been helping to serve the refreshments became indisposed and had to be assisted to a small ante-room, or cludgie as it is called. To my horror I learned that she had inadvertently swallowed a portion of a valuable necklace. Several of my fellow-guests informed me, "She has a good bead in her."

I was relieved when, some thirty minutes later, the lady reappeared and intimated with what I took to be a Glaswegian medical term that she had made a complete recovery. "AGOATITAWUP," she disclosed. Them to my astonishment, she made an announcement that no doubt survives from the Roman occupation of old Scotia. In fluent Latin she proclaimed, "O SEEZA SLUGATRAT BOATLARUM!"

But yet another mishap occurred. From an adjoining apartment came an agonised female shriek followed by an urgent pronouncement in the strange argot of Rasooside . . . "DRAPTIZ! DRAPTIZ BOATTLE OAN MA FIT!" My surmise that something untoward had happened proved only too true when I was informed that the hostess was having her first fit in the kitchen.

My alarm was increased when a lady who had been gazing from a window turned white-faced to the gathering and in a voice that trembled with fear gave them the dread news that a symbolical harbinger of ill-fortune was about to visit them. "Black Maria is coming!" she wailed.

The very name struck terror into the Hogmanay celebrants. "Black Maria is coming!" they cried as, panic-stricken, they began to flee from the house. In vain did I endeavour to calm their superstitious fears. "Fear not!" I adjured them, "I shall face up to Black Maria!" One comely maiden expressed her warm approval of my proposal. In her fascinating Highland tongue she wished me well with the haunting words — "OCHAWAN! ... OCHAWAN! ... OCHAWANGIT-STUFT!"

Parliamo Glasgow

Dining Out

LECTURER:	Some picturesque examples of the native language may be heard in certain Glasgow eating houses. We begin this lesson with an excerpt from my play "STUFFINYURTURKI", or in English. "DINING OUT".
Seated at a table in a modest cafe a young man awaits the arrival of a damsel with whom he has formed a romantic attachment. A waitress approaches and regards him with disapproval.
WAITRESS:	(ASIDE) Aw, ra bliddy pest! (TO THE YOUNG MAN) Whiddje fur?
YOUNG MAN:	Nuhin ra noo. Waitin' fur a burd. (HE TAKES A CIGARETTE STUB FROM BEHIND HIS EAR) Er, goarra . . . goarra li'?

THE WAITRESS TAKES A BOX OF MATCHES FROM HER APRON POCKET AND HANDS IT TO HIM. THE YOUNG MAN

Portrait of a high-powered female business executive, the kind of glossy American career lady featured in glossy American magazines.

STRIKES A MATCH. BUT, WHILE GAZING AT THE WAITRESS'S BUST, HE BECOMES DISTRAIT. HE THROWS DOWN THE MATCH SUDDENLY.

AWGORRA nearly burnt ma snitch aff! THE GIRL ARRIVES AND SEATS HERSELF AT THE TABLE.

GIRL:	Yur therr.
YOUNG MAN:	Whirra hell kep' ye?
GIRL:	Zootra messidges fur ma murra. Bought hur a punna fresh burra.
YOUNG MAN:	A punna burra furra murra? Could yur wee brurra no' go furra punna burra furra? Or yur urra brurra?
GIRL:	Huvny goarra anurra brurra.
YOUNG MAN:	Aw your bahookie!
GIRL:	(LOOKING ROUND AT HER BOTTOM) 'Supwit?
YOUNG MAN:	Shut yur geggie. (TO WAITRESS) The usual.
WAITRESS:	Pies is aff.
GIRL:	Can Ah've a curry?
YOUNG MAN:	(TO WAITRESS) Curry fur ra burd.
WAITRESS:	S'nuttoan.
YOUNG MAN:	(SNATCHING MENU CARD FROM WAITRESS AND GLARING AT IT) Thur hee-haw oan! Ma goarra never seen the like. 'Saw aff! . . . We're aff an' a'!

THE YOUNG MAN AND THE

GIRL RISE AND LEAVE THE
CAFE.

*   *   *   *

LECTURER: Let me translate and explain the deli-
cate nuances of the words and
phrases used in the cafe, or Tally's as
we call it. When the young man arrives
to dine he does not hear the waitress's
sotto voce observation —
AURABLIDDIPEST
This word is traditionally voiced by
waitresses in eating houses to indi-
cate that the establishment is about to
close for the night and the prospective
diner is not wholly welcome . . . Nevertheless, the waitress endeavours to
ascertain the customer's require-
ments with the simple query . . .
WHIDDJEFUR?
Note the prefix "WHIDDJE". We use
this generally in the imperative sense,
that is, when asking an important
question. Accordingly, a young lady
may say to her escort, or lumbur,
WHIDDJEWAANT?
WHIDDJEDAEN?
WHIDDJEHINKA UM?
Of course, if the lumbur is unduly
amorous the maiden may reinforce
her inquiry with the more emphatic
phrase . . .

Overleaf: As Rex Harrison.

NUNNARAT . . . CURRITOOT!

But that is by the way . . . In the cafe the young man intimates to the waitress that he will postpone his repast. He employs a word that has no doubt been borrowed from our Pakistani citizens . . .

NUHINRANU

When he inadvertently burns his nose with a match while surveying the waitress's physique he exclaims . . .

AWGOARRA NEARLY BURNT MA SNITCH AFF!

You may have noticed that the young man has more than once used the word . . .

GOARRA

When asking for the means to light his cigarette he said . . .

GOARRALI?

"GOARRA" is often used when we are making a request or seeking information. So we have . . .

GOARRA NEW NEEBUR?
GOARRA STORY ABOOT HUR?
GOARRA DEKATUR FANCIMAN?

When "GOARRA" is prefixed by the syllable "AW" it changes its meaning entirely. Here are some examples . . .

AWGOARRA PIPE'S BURSTIT?
AWGOARRA CEILIN'S FELL IN!
AWGOARRA WIFE'S MURRA'S

HERE!

But back to the cafe. The young lady enters and expresses her joy at seeing the lumbur with the rather charming greeting the Glasgow damsel reserves for her lover . . .

YURTHERR

Her sweetheart is concerned that she might have lost her way and he inquires solicitously . . .

WHIRRAHELKEPYI?

The young lady reveals that she has been purchasing a pound of butter for her mother, or as she puts it . . .

APUNNABURRAFURRAMURRA

The word "FURRA" confuses most English people and other foreigners. It has several meanings — all relating to romance. A gentleman studying a photograph of a young lady in Playboy magazine might sigh . . .

OFURRANIGHTWIHUR!

A young lady wishing to curtail the activities of a passionate lover would also use the word "FURRA" as she informed him . . .

YURGAUNAEFURRA

In the cafe, you may remember, the lumbur cut short the lovers' tiff with the cryptic utterance . . .

AWYURBAHOOKIE

This was merely an ancient word that

signified the discussion was at an end. But, such are the subtleties of the language, even the young Glasgow lady misunderstood him. She believed he was being critical of the rear portion of her anatomy. So she demands to know . . .

SUPWIT?

Her escort, however, simply advises her to preserve a dignified silence. He uses one of our age-old phrases . . .

SHUTYUR GEGGIE

He could have conveyed his request by employing a variety of delightful words, such as . . .

ACHSHURRIT

CLEYUP

GIEYURJAWAREST

and

PIRRASOACKINIT

However, the young man goes on to ask the waitress to serve their usual dinner. She responds with a word obviously borrowed from the Russian language . . .

PYZIZAFF

Prompted by his inamorata, he orders another dish . . .

CURRIFURRABURD

When the young gentleman discovers that there is little or nothing listed on the menu card he ends the visit to the cafe with the trenchant declaration . . .

SAWAFFANWEERAFFANAW!

The Professor on

Mating Habits

On a recent visit to the great metropolis on the Clyde I was fortunate enough to witness the strange ritual courtship engaged in by certain of the young natives.

In a busy thoroughfare I took note of two young maidens, or "burds", guardedly scrutinising a pair of young males who had come into view. The young braves flaunted their gaily-coloured raiment and hair arranged in spikes and made their presence known to the females with the plaintive cry . . .

HEH-HINGMI!

The word "HING-MI" plays no small part in the conversation of the natives whose desire it is to mate. Indeed, from one of the colourful males I heard it used in the plural . . .

HINGMIZ

Gazing fondly upon one of the damsels who was extremely well-proportioned he uttered the haunting love-call . . .

SHIHUZSUMPERRAHINGMIZ

I took it that he was referring to the lustrous eyes of the young lady. She at once replied to his call with the Gaelic word . . .

OCHONE

A favourite impression, that of Mrs Bridges, the unforgett-able cook in the TV series "Upstairs, Downstairs."

embellishing it with the pretty expression . . .

YURWEY YANYUK

And so the full beauty of her answering call came to me . . .

OCHONE YURWEY YANYUK!

With eyes shyly averted the maidens continued on their way. Then the other male adolescent delivered himself of the manly mating-cry . . .

GONNIGEESE

He was obviously likening the two "burds" to those of the feathered variety. He continued his ornithological theme with . . .

GONNIGEESE ADATEHEN?

The objects of their affection appeared to heed not the urgent cries. It seemed to me as if the courtship were doomed to failure. Then suddenly one of the prepossessing maidens turned round to face the wooers. From her lips came the romantic love-call that doubtless has echoed down the Highland glens from time immemorial. It began with the exotic-sounding . . .

AWAYNGIT

and was completed with the monosyllabic . . .

WAASHT

so that the love-call in its entirety was . . .

AWAYNGITWAASHT

Ah, what ecstasy there was in the voices of the two young males as they responded to the young lady's heartfelt request. Triumphantly they demonstrated their joy with exultant chorus . . .

YAPERRA! YAPERRA!

YAPERRAHERRIES!

As the two maidens were vanishing into the Keltic

twilight they continued to call encouragement to their eager suitors. Their sweet girlish voices were raised in an old Caledonian love-song which began with the word . . .

YIZZIZZA

I listened entranced as the poetic invitation filled the night air with its lyrical loveliness . . .
YIZZIZZACUPLADAMGOATS,
YIZZIZZACUPLABAMPOATS.

Delighted, the two young cavaliers replied with great fervour . . .
AWGUIDRIDDINZ,
YAPERRAMIDDINZ!

Parliamo Glasgow

Consumer Affairs

LECTURER: The rich Glaswegian language is heard at its most beautiful when native speakers are discussing consumer affairs. We illustrate this lesson with an introductory playlet in which we see a young lady and her fiancé making various purchases in a supermarket.

*   *   *   *

YOUNG LADY: Wherra hell did you get tae?

FIANCÉ: Did ye no' see me at the wine coonter?

YOUNG LADY: 'Sat yuv goat therr?

FIANCÉ: 'Sa boa' 'la scud. Gi'es ye a rerr glow. (HE PUTS BOTTLE IN HER BASKET AND TAKES FROM IT A JAR OF JELLY) . . . Whissis ye've goat, Mattie?

YOUNG LADY: 'Sa jaura jeelly. FIANCÉ PUTS THE JAR OF JELLY

Starring as that eminent star-gazer, Patrick Moore.

BACK IN BASKET.
YOUNG LADY TAKES PURSE
FROM BASKET, PUTS BASKET ON
FLOOR AND RUMMAGES
THROUGH PURSE.

YOUNG LADY: Ah'm a bit shoart.

FIANCÉ: Ah know . . . Ye're wee but gemme.

YOUNG LADY: Ah need a p.

FINANCÉ: It's aw rat shandy ye hud.

YOUNG LADY: Ya bampoat! 'Sa PENNY Ah need!

FIANCÉ: (TAKING JAR OF PÂTÉ from basket) Heh, whissis?

YOUNG LADY: 'Sa jaura pait.

FIANCÉ; Ye don't cry it "pait" . . . It's "pâté", Mattie.

YOUNG LADY: Then why huv thae pit "pate" oan the jaur fur?

FIANCÉ: 'Cos the French don't say "pait". They say "pâté", Mattie.

YOUNG LADY: Well Ah'm no' French . . . Ah've ate pait an' a wee tait o' pait oan a plate's great wi' a pataity.

FIANCÉ; Ye're batty, Mattie. Rat pâté wi' a tattie'll mak ye a fatty, Mattie.

*   *   *   *

LECTURER: Let us study the conversational exchanges between the young lady and her fiancé, or "hur intendit" as he is called, in the supermarket.

When the young lady, Mattie, discovers that her fiancé has strayed from her side she uses the well-known Glaswegian word . . .

JIJU

To it she puts the prefix . . .

WHERRAHEL

Then she adds . . .

GERRY

And so she inquires of the young gentleman . . .

WHERRAHELJIJUGERRY?

a lady seeking her husband's aid on finding that the glass containing her dentures has vanished from her bed-side table will preface her query with the word . . .

JIJU

adding a few more syllables to it to give us . . .

JIJUSEEMAWALLISKICKINA-BOOT?

to which her husband may well reply . . .

JIJUNOPITREMOANRAMANTEL-PIECE?

When the young lady in the super-market observes that her fiancé is in possession of a bottle she addresses him with the Russian-sounding word . . .

SATYUV

to which she appends . . .

GOATRERR

thus completing the question . . .

SATYUVGOATRERR?

The young gentleman discloses that he has visited the wine department from which he has selected a bottle of wine or, as he puts it, . . .

BOALASCUD

He gives his opinion of its quality with the technical expression . . .

GEEZYARERRGLO

As he places the bottle in the wire basket he displays an interest in the contents of the latter. He takes from the basket one of the purchases and questions the damsel about it. In her explanation she borrows from the Spanish language and says . . .

SAJORRA

SAJORRAJEELI

At this juncture the young lady discovers that she does not quite have the sum required as payment for her groceries. She informs her escort . . .

AMSHOART

He, believing that she is referring to her diminutive stature, pays her a graceful compliment . . .

YURWEEBUTGEMME

But the maiden has no time for compliments. She points out that she needs one penny or, in the colloquial parlance, "a p." Once again her "intendit" misunderstands her. He contends that certain refreshments she has consumed have discommoded her. Employing what would appear to be an Indian word, he alleges . . .

SAWRATSHANDIYEHUD

The young lady hotly refutes the suggestion. Meanwhile the fiancé extracts another of her purchases from the basket and desires her to idenitfy it. Again she uses the Spanish word
. . .

SAJORRA
SAJORRAPAIT

Her companion ruminates over her use of the word "pait". Then he realises her mistake and corrects her with two trenchant words . . .

SNOPAIT, SPATTIMATTI

His fiancé resents his criticism and declines to adopt the French pronunciation. She goes on to extol the appetising nature of the product. In syllables of the purest poesy she assures him . . .

A V A T E P A I T A N A W E E T A I T A-
PAITOANAPLATESGREATWIAPA-
TAITY

The young man is fearful of the dire effect this culinary melange will have on his loved one's girth. He questions

her sanity in eating pâté with potato
and cries out the warning . . .
YURBATTIMATTI RATPATTI-
WIATATTIALMAKYEAFATTI-
MATTI!

The Professor at a

Hallowe'en Party

My semantical and anthropological research obliged me to pay yet another visit to the great city of Glasgow. To me its fascination derives from the aura of Keltic mysticism that pervades it.

Accordingly I was all agog when, on visiting one of the city's quaint old hostelries, or "boozers" as they are termed, I met a gentleman who appeared to be completely au fait with the customs and language of his native habitat.

He spoke of a strange mystic rite which was to be performed that very evening in the remote clan stronghold of Castle Milk.

"To whom," I enquired, "is this ceremony dedicated?"

"Sally Een," my companion revealed.

I had not heard of Sally Een but I concluded that she was one of those enchanting figures with which the folklore of Old Scotia is so richly endowed. Not so well-known, perhaps, as those other legendary heroines, Mesdames Fran and Anna, La Lulu and the tragic lady known as Auntie Mary who had such trouble with her recalcitrant canary.

Too scantily clad as Miss Autumn. Net result — a bad cold.

I intimated to my new-found friend that I was more than anxious to pay tribute to Sally Een. Lapsing into his native Glasgois, he uttered an explanation of surprise . . .

"SAPERTI!"

Then impulsively he issued the invitation . . .

"'SUP AT RA FANCY WUMMAN'S!"

I assured him that I would be honoured to sup at the abode of The Fancy Wumman. I particularly desired to meet the high priestess who was to officiate at the Ceremony of Sally Een. Without further ado we proceeded to the gathering-place.

The door of the house was opened by a lady whom I at once recognised as The Fancy Wumman. Her multi-coloured hair was garnished with picturesque metal cylinders and her face was painted in vivid shades of white and red.

She greeted my escort by name, crying . . .

IT'S SAUL!

IT'S SAUL SODYHEID!

Quickly Mr Sodyheid whispered to her what I took to be a Gaelic password . . .

ERRAKERRYOOT

Thereupon The Fancy Wumman relieved me of the large paper container filled with bottles and cans which custom had obliged me to purchase in the hostelry. Then we joined the participants in the tribal rite. Already the solemn proceedings had commenced.

A comely damsel was kneeling upon a chair. She was in the act of causing a fork to fall from her lips into a sacrificial font filled with water in which floated a quantity of apples. There was a tense silence as the symbolic fork descended quickly to the bottom of the font.

The young lady gazed down in pious meditation at the apples, then, throwing back her head, she gave vent to an incantation . . .

RADAMPT! RADAMPTFOARKSBLUNTASBUGRI!

Next an aged gentleman declared that he too wished to play his part in the awe-inspiring ritual. I was greatly moved by the devoutness in his tones as he proclaimed . . .

HERESHOOTI! HERESHOOTI DOOKFURAIPPLES!

With tender care the other devotees of Sally Een assisted the patriarch to kneel upon the chair. Reverently the handle of the fork was placed between his lips. A moment later came a clattering sound from the font. The old gentleman looked up, toothless, and from all sides came the inspiring chorus of acclamation . . .

IZWALLIZFELOOTWIRRAFOARK!

I observed other touching acts of devotion at the gathering.

One of these, it transpired, called for a statuesque maiden wearing an abbreviated skirt to seat herself upon a large specially-prepared scone which had been placed on an armchair. She then rose quickly and uttered a traditional call first heard centuries ago during the Franco-Scottish alliance . . .

MERCI!

She at once added another word to give the elaborate incantation . . .

MERCIZAWTRAICLE!

The ceremonial continued in all its Caledonian majesty and reached a triumphant climax when the lady known as The Fancy Wumman plunged headfirst into the water amongst the apples. This was the signal for the other participants in the celebration to hail her as their goddess. They chorused fervently . . .

GODDESS! GODDESS!

GODDESS MUNSE SINCE SHE HUDDA WAASH!

The solemn observances came to an end when the devotees of Sally Een assumed their grotesque tribal masks or, as their patois has it, "fause faces".

I made bold to congratulate the young lady in the short skirt on her mask. "Never," I assured her, "have I seen such a repulsive countenance". Graciously, in the lilting language of her island forefathers, she acknowledged my felicitations concerning her "fause face". She trilled . . .

GOARUMNO

GOARUMNO WERRINWAN!

When eventually I took my departure she bade my farewell with the charming Gaelic words . . .

YAULSCUNNUR YURAFFYURRUDDICHUMP!

Parliamo Glasgow

The Contretemps

LECTURER:	Some of the most intriguing words in the lovely lilting language of Glasgow are heard when natives of the city become involved in some sort of contretemps. This fact may be demonstrated in the playlet we use for this lesson.
	The locale is a street and there a buxom maiden is in attendance at a barrow from which she is selling a variety of fruit and vegetables.
	A young man known as THE FLYFELLA enters.
FLY FELLA:	(LOOKING BEHIND HIM) Whirra hell's ra marra?
	HIS SWEETHEART, OR BURD, ENTERS. SHE IS FATIGUED AND HER FEET APPEAR TO BE CAUSING HER SOME DIS-COMFORT.
BURD:	An canny go nae farra.
FLY FELLA:	Here Clarra wi' hur barra! Take a

A soupcon of suspicion from that terrifying 'tec, Philip Marlowe.

	sate oan ra haun'le o' ra barra.
BURD:	'Stoo narra.
FLY FELLA:	So 'tis. (GLANCING AT BURD'S REAR) That's some jaxi ye've oan ye!
BURD:	'Sno' as big as your heid.
	BOTH SURVEY THE FRUIT ON THE BARROW. THE FLY FELLA FINGERS TWO MELONS.
BARROW-GIRL:	Haun's aff ra melons!
FLY FELLA:	Ah never laid a finger oan ye! (HE NOTICES A MARROW) Heh, zarra marra oan yur barra, Clarra?
BARROW-GIRL:	(SARCASTICALLY) 'Sno' a tamarra.
FLY FELLA:	(POINTING TO GROUND) A tamarra's tummul't ootra barra, Clarra.
BURD:	Ah think Ah'll buy ra marra fur ma farra. Mia Farra bought a marra fur hur farra.
FLY FELLA:	S'ootra question. Whit's YOUR farra waant wi' a marra affa barra?
	BURD PICKS UP THE MARROW
BARROW-GIRL:	(SHOUTS) Pirrat marra back!
	BURD, STARTLED, DROPS THE MARROW ON THE BARROW. THE BARROW GOES OVER WITH A CRASH.
FLY FELLA:	Aw, Mia Farra's cowped Clarra's barra wi' a marra!

64

LECTURER: Some of the words and phrases used in the playlet may sound strange to non-Glaswegians. The Fly Fella betrays some anxiety about the young lady with whom he has been strolling. He wishes to know what is troubling her and inquires solicitously . . .

WHIRRA HELZA MARRA?

Note the key-word . . .

HELZA

This is frequently heard at social functions. Thus . . .

WHENRA HELZA PERTY STERTIN'?

WHYRA HELZA BURDS NO' HERE?

WHERRA HELZA BOOZE?

But back to our playlet. You may recall that the Fly Fella made an interesting allusion to the rearward contours of the young lady's anatomy, observing "That's some jaxi ye've oan ye!"

YU-VOAN-YE

This introduces to us the descriptive words . . .

VOAN, ZOAN and TOAN

These invariably relate to the physiological aspects of a person. A young man-about-town commenting on the physical attributes of a

---

Overleaf: Miss Heartburn as she appeared in that Broadway medical musical.

young lady will say . . .

SOMEBOADISHE ZOAN UR!

But his friend, more fastidious than he, might exclaim . . .

LUKATRAFA TOAN UR!

And, of course, there is the phrase often used when a Glaswegian native is confronted by an unusually rotund lady or gentleman . . .

WHIRRAKYTEYU VOAN YE!

Now we come to the rather dramatic part of our playlet — when the Fly Fella discovers the vegetable marrow reposing in the barrow. At once he utters the lovely phrase . . .

ZARRA MARRA OANRA BARRA CLARRA?

Remember "ZARRA" is employed when we wish to find out something, as in . . .

ZARRA FACMAC?

Meaning — "Is that the case, stranger?" Sometimes we may be confused as to a person's identity. Again we use "ZARRA". A long-haired individual in a dimly-lit discotheque might occasion the query . . .

ZARRA CHICKORRA HERRIWULLI?

Again, an amorous damsel could

use the word romatically to her bashful lover . . .

ZARRA BESYEKINDAE?

Next I want to draw your attention to another charming word. It was used when the Fly Fella noticed that a tomato had fallen from the fruit barrow . . .

A TAMARRA'S TUMMUL-TOOTRA BARRA!

The important word here is . . .

TUMMUL-TOOTRA

We also have . . .

TUMMUL-TINTERA

A lady who had been accidentlly precipitated into a rubbish depository may be said to have . . .

TUMMUL-TINTERA MIDDIN

But we have many words bearing the prefix . . .

TUMMUL

such as . . .

TUMMUL-TAFFRA

A gentleman who met with a mishap after dining and wining would be reported as having . . .

TUMMUL-TAFFRA CHERR

A word new in our vocabulary stems from the permissive society. Referring to a lady and gentleman meeting for the first time we make use of . . .

TUMMUL-TINTY

To this we add the Latin word . . .

RAPERRAREM

And so we have the interesting statement . . .

RAPERRAREM TUMMUL-TINTY BED

When the young lady in the playlet wishes to purchase the marrow for her father her escort tells her brusquely . . .

SOOTRA QUESTION

The word . . .

SOOTRA

would be heard from the young lady if she came to realise that the ungallant Fly Man was not a suitable associate for her. She would preface it with the word . . .

YURBUM

She would then deliver herself of the trenchant declaration that has come from the lips of many a Glaswegian maiden disillusioned with her male acquaintance . . .

YURBUMSOOTRAWINDAE!

The Professor attends

A Wedding Reception

I had deemed it no small honour that the members of a learned society should ask me to address them on the fruits of my Glasgovian researches. Alas, Fate ordained that I should not appear before the distinguished gathering. By a complete mischance I found myself in a different edifice from that which I had intended to visit.

To a gentleman standing at the portals I confessed that I had lost my bearings. To my surprise he clapped me upon the shoulder and with the utmost good humour declared . . .

AH, MISTA WEY!

I, of course, informed him that I was not Mr Wey. The gentleman, however, did not appear to hear me. In the strange but appealing argot of the Eastern province of Brigton he bade me a cordial welcome, crying . . .

JEEZYURSTOCIOUS!

and forthwith he marched me triumphantly into the hall. Great was my astonishment and delight when I perceived that I was attending a highly-important Scottish ceremony . . .

THE FEAST OF RAWADDIN

Yes, it was a typical Scottish wedding fiesta. With the

Double impersonation — as Charlton Heston as Moses in the film epic.

other celebrants I awaited the arrival of the newly-espoused couple. A gasp of surprise arose when the bride entered unaccompanied or, in the native idiom . . .

OANURBLIDDITOD

Some concern was shown by the matriarch of the bride's clan, a venerable lady who was referred to by her title . . .

HURAULGRANNI

In a voice that rang through the hall the matriarch called . . .

WHERRAHELZAGROOM

In accordance with custom she was answered by a diminutive gentleman known variously by the company as . . .

RABBESMAN or
BOWLIWEEBACHLE

He revealed the whereabouts of the bridegroom. In a charming old Gaelic rhyme he announced . . .

RABUGGRULNOBUDGE
OOTRABLOOMINCLUDGE

It transpired that the bridegroom had been overcome by emotion and had retired to an ante-room. But in less than an hour he appeared, pale and a little unsteady in his gait. Once again came a call from . . .

HURAULGRANNI

She welcomed the young man to the company, calling him by what appeared to be her pet name for him . . .

GLAIKITNYAFF

What pride was in her tones as she hailed him with . . .

GLAIKITNYAFF YURBEVVID!

Next came the ceremonial partitioning of the wedding cake. With grave demeanour the newly-wedded damsel took up a large knife and inserted it in the impressive confection. Then softly from her lips came a mystic incantation, a plea for connubial bliss that doubtless her ancestors had voiced many centuries before . . .

HORDUZ!
HORDUZ ABLIDDIBRICK!

To assist her in the solemn rite the bridegroom, whose name I gathered was "Pete", placed his hand over that of his bride. I was deeply moved when she looked shyly at her nuptial partner and made to him what was obviously an age-old pledge of devotion . . .

FURRALUVVAPETE
YURHAUNZASWEET

It was not long ere I became aware of another participant in the ceremonies. I understood her name to be . . .

HURMURRA

She listened intently as a gentleman raised his glass in a toast to the bride and bridegroom. In his native language he intoned . . .

GUIDLUCKYIZZILNEEDIT!

At this juncture the lady known as . . .

HURMURRA

bent her head in silent prayer. She then commenced a tribal chant in praise of the sweetness of the married state. What sincerity there was in her voice as she sang . . .

O MOLASSES! O MOLASSES!

I was quick to note the aptness of the word as she continued with the lovely old ballad . . .

O MOLASSESMERRITAHEIDCASE!

Overwhelmed by the sentimental nature of the occasion the bride became faint and was helped to a chair.

So affected was she that she did not know the name of the establishment in which the wedding celebration was being held. Tremulously she asked . . .
WHERRUMMA?
   Without hesitation the information was given to her by . . .
HURMURRA
   She began with the obscure word . . .
YURINRA
   Then she added a word that made everything clear to the bride. Gaily she cried . . .
YURINRA PUDNCLUB!

Thespians in Trouble

English producers, actresses and actors may encounter certain difficulties when endeavouring to present Scottish plays in the theatre or on television.

This is illustrated in the following sketch in which some people from south of the Border are seen rehearsing Part I of a Scottish drama series for television.

SCENE: A television studio somewhere in Scotland;

CAST: *BASIL*, an English producer;
          AUBREY, and English actor;
          BRENDA, an English actress;
          GLASGOW GIRL

         *   *   *   *

BASIL: Well, let's get going . . . You'll notice the action takes place in the Scotch highlands, round about Falkirk, or some such village. Now we've got to bring out the undertones of Keltic tragedy and the mystique of the Gaelic character.

AUBREY: Basil, I'm not awfully sure about some of the words . . .

Television debut as Cinderella.

BASIL: Not sure? Damn it all, Aubrey, you should
            know the Scotch lingo by this time! You've
            been a whole week in Glasgow . . . Let's
            do the scene with Brenda and you in the
            West End.

BRENDA: (PEERING AT HER SCRIPT) It says here
            "SINGLE-end".

BASIL: Yes . . . Well, that'll be their name for the
            West End. We're in a bothy — that's some
            sort of castle — and there's an open fire
            with porridge, bannocks and whatnot boil-
            ing away in a pot. In a corner of the lounge
            sits an old Gaelic crone.

BRENDA: That's me.

BASIL: Yes, you're Morag. She has a clan title,
            Morag the Toerag . . . Now, where are
            we? Ah yes. Su-mass, her son, goes to
            the window . . . Go on, Aubrey.

AUBREY: (GOES TO WINDOW AND READS
            FROM SCRIPT) "The tatties are biling all
            over the range" . . . Basil, what exactly are
            tatties?

BASIL: Eh? . . . Oh . . . er . . . they're birds of
            ill-omen, like albatrosses, you know. So I
            think you should be terror-stricken as you
            look out on the moor and see the tatties
            wheeling about.

AUBREY: I see . . . "The tatties are biling all over the
            range" . . . Do they have ranges in Scot-
            land?

BASIL: Never mind that . . . Brenda, you show
            you're frightened too.

80

BRENDA:	Oh yes . . . "Ockone! Ockone! I am terrible!" Oh, sorry . . . "I am terrible fee-art!"
BASIL:	Go on, Aubrey. You try to comfort her.
AUBREY:	(TO BRENDA) "Do not bother your ginger, hen.
BASIL:	(CALLS TO SIDE OF STAGE) I say, have you got the ginger hen?
	GLASGOW GIRL ENTERS AND SHOWS HIM A BROWN HEN.
	Good, good. (TO AUBREY AND BRENDA) The ginger hen is another symbolic bird. But we don't need it yet. (TO GIRL) Put it in my office.
	GIRL EXITS WITH HEN
	(TO AUBREY) You go back to the window, Aubrey. You feel that some frightful catastrophe is going to happen. Go on.
AUBREY:	(READING) "Er . . . the lickt is fading fast and I canna see my brither's boattie on the lock."
BASIL:	Come ON, Brenda!
BRENDA:	Just a sec . . . Ah, here we are. (READS) "Wae is me! Me laddeh is drooned in the lock! Me laddeh who was to have wad Flora Col-cue-hown. She wad have been sick . . ."
BASIL:	Surely not SICK!
BRENDA:	Sorry! . . . "She wad have been sic a prood bride, a gay prood bride."
BASIL:	Just a moment. Gay prude bride? I don't quite understand how she could be gay AND a prude . . . Oh well, go on.

Overleaf: As the celebrated Film Maker Zokol. "This role put years on me." says Stanley.

BRENDA:	"There will be nae wadding now . . . er . . . noo, nae C. Liddell. Me laddeh aye liked to gang to C.Liddell's . . ."
AUBREY:	Basil, who is this character, C. Liddell?
BASIL:	(IMPATIENTLY) It's not a character. It's a sea-lid — C.E.I.L.I.D.H. Some sort of game the Scotch peasants play . . . Please, let's get on with it! Aubrey, I want you to . . .

GLASGOW GIRL ENTERS

GIRL:	Hey Jimmy.
BASIL:	How dare you interrupt me in the middle of a rehearsal!
GIRL:	Keep ra heid, Mac.
AUBREY:	What on earth is she saying?
BASIL:	I've no idea WHAT she's saying. (TO GIRL) What do you want?
GIRL:	Nuchin' . . . Thur a fulla oana phone fur ye.
BASIL:	What IS she saying?
BRENDA:	It's Greek to me!
GIRL:	Ya shoo'ra chancers, diz nane o' yiz un-nerstaun' plain English?

The Professor Pays

A Tribute to Rabbie

In a Glasgovian tavern I was refreshing myself with that delightful Scottish drink, a "hoffannahoff", when a venerable native scholar hailed me with a salutation which survives from the time of the Roman occupation of his country. He cried . . .

O CAESAR!

To this he added a word to give me the splendid greeting in full . . .

O CAESARAFIVER

He gave me to understand that on payment of £5 I could be a guest at a supper party in honour of a Scottish literary gentleman by the name of "Rabbie".

I was discomfited at having to confess that I had not heard of Mr Rabbie. Great was my astonishment when my aged acquaintance intimated to me that Mr Rabbie had been corresponding with a Canadian quadruped. Yes, he disclosed, "Rabbie wrote to a moose." I ventured to inquire if he had received a reply to his epistle; but the gentleman was reticent on the subject. He looked at me solemnly and intoned . . .

TWIDGIEYIRABOAK

Without further ado the aged scholar and I repaired to

Another role that put years on him — The Mad Scientist.

the literary salon where we were to pay tribute to the illustrious Mr Rabbie.

Seated at a long table in the salon was a concourse of erudite gentlemen. Already they were proposing toasts to various Scottish men of letters, such as Mr Poosie Nancy, Messrs Birks of Aberfeldy and an author of Irish descent, Mr Tam O'Shanter.

Not a few of the guests present were apparently of Russian origin. On all sides were mentioned the names . . .

AMFURRAHOFF, GIEZAHOFF and SEEZAHOFF

A guest who kept leaving the company precipitately then returning bore the impressive Slavonic cognomen . . .

MOSCOW TAERALAVVI

The carnival of Caledonian culture continued with a gaiety that was contagious. Loud and long came the celebratory cries that have made the rafters ring at many an assemblage of the Scottish intelligentsia . . .
WHERRZAWINE? MAGLESSIZEMPY!
AMBEVVID! PETESPUKIN!

I made so bold as to inquire of the chairman as to when we might expect the arrival of Mr Rabbie. A sudden deep silence ensued and all eyes were upon me. Then, to my unutterable gratification, the chairman solemnly conferred on me an ancient Highland title. "You," he declared, "are the real Chieftain of the Pudden Race". So saying, he urged that the distinguished guests should all heed me, crying in ringing tones . . .
AULHEIDCASE!

A few minutes later I again had cause to marvel at the cosmopolitan nature of the gathering. A request for silence came from a diminutive gentleman, or wee bachle as he was known to the cognoscenti present. He announced his intention of regaling us with what I understood to be an Indian song . . .

RASH TARA

To my regret the singer was so overcome by the poignancy of the Eastern ballad that he was able only to give voice to one haunting line . . .

RASH TARA RABBIBURNS

Nevertheless my supper companions showed their appreciation of his gallant effort with the appropriate Indian felicitation . . .

IZDENCHURZ HUZFELOOT

Soon came the strains of the bagpipes. But the bagpiper too found the grandeur of the occasion too much for him. He had some difficulty in amassing sufficient wind for his instrument. But the chairman rose and proudly identified the bagpiper for us, proclaiming . . .

HE IS STOCIOUS

Carried away by the sheer pageantry of the spectacle I too greeted the bagpiper with a hearty . . .

HAIL, MR STOCIOUS!

Unfortunately, in my enthusiasm, I jolted the arm of a stout gentleman in cook's attire. Thereupon a large grey sphere he was carrying before him on a salver flew through the air and disintegrated on the chairman's countenance. From the onlookers came excited exclamations of . . .

IZDRAPTRABLIDDIHAGGIS!

With that came the ritual that terminated the literary evening. A gentleman with the word "Hallkeeper"

emblazoned on his headgear made his entrance. In a
stentorian voice he called . . .

OOTRALOTOYIZ! OOTORALGETRAPOLIS!

And as we poured from the premises into the friendly
darkness of the Glasgwegian night we could hear him
giving us the old Gaelic blessing . . .

YASHOORASOAKS! GOADPEETIYIZ!

Grammar

That Has Went into

Desuetude

Such are the passionate nationalistic feelings of many Glaswegians that English grammar and pronunciation are often altered and sometimes ignored by them. This is exemplified in the traditional love ballad . . .

FABULACIOUS CREACHER
The most loveliest girl I ever seen
Had came into my life.
My eyes was quick to see this queen . . .
Oh that she'd be my wife!
But I could never reach her,
This fabulacious creacher.

Her hair more blacker than the night,
Her eyes most deepest blue,
I'd never saw more sweeter sight,
But from my gaze she's flew.
Oh how I love each feacher
Of this fabulacious creacher.

When first I seen this lovely maid
I knowed that I had fell

Of course, the real Carol Channing is much prettier.

In love with one who'd made the grade,
An intylectuel.
But I could not never reacher,
The fabulacious creacher.

I begged her for to be my bride.
(I'd went down on my knees).
Alas, she run quick from my side
And learnt my heart to freeze.
Oh if only I could meet yer,
You fabulacious creacher!

But now I've went and gave up hope;
My loved one's went away.
She's never wrote and so I mope
And render this sad lay.

I just can't never reach 'er,
This fabulacious creacher,
The most beautifullest girl,
My lovely English teacher.

From

the Concise Parliamo Dictionary

of Current Glaswegian

The following list of the more obscure Glaswegian words and phrases with approximate definitions in ordinary English may be of some use to non-Scots who visit the great cultural metropolis on the Clyde.

SHURSEL, HULLAWRERR, YURTHERR: Words of greeting.
GOARA, used in various contexts, as follows —
GOARAMDRI, an acute thirst has assailed me.
GOARAFAGOANYE, a request for a cigarette.
GOARAHELL, used when declining to give the importunate person a cigarette.

Various terms are used by the natives when discussing the vagaries of the weather.
SWAARMRADAY, the temperature has risen.
RASUNZOOT! a miracle has taken place!
SPELTINARAIN, we have returned to normal climatic conditions.
SELLUVAKOLNOO, the temperature has now fallen.
MASPUDZIZFROZE, my feet are extremely cold.

Many Glaswegians seek their holiday pleasures abroad. Foreign doctors might find it advisable to acquaint themselves with some of the terms used in describing the symptoms of various ailments.
MADIALZBEALIN, Some skin is no longer adhering to my face.
MACHAMPURZIZBROON, Even my dentures are sunburnt.
AVAHEIDANAHOF, The modestly-priced wine is stronger than I thought.
AVASERRKYTE, I am suffering from stomach pains.

AMOFFI PEELIWALLI, The large seafood meal I ate has made me feel somewhat frail.

ASATOANA DAUDAGLESS, I failed to notice the broken wine bottle before I sat down on the beach.

On their return from a sojourn in mainland Spain or Majorca many Glasgow natives display their snapshots with pride. Expressions that accompany their photographic exhibition are —

WANNISEE WURPHOTIES? Can I induce you to suffer an hour of extreme boredom?

ERRMAMURRAPAIDLIN, That is a study of my mother seeking a sea-water easement of her painful corns.

WEEFELLA BELLAFELLINWI, A small gentleman who took Bella out in a pedalo which capsized.

RAWEANFLINGIN SAUNABOOT, the child merrily throwing sand about.

SKELPINFURRAWEAN, Father cutting short the child's enjoyment.

MAWYELLINHURHEIDAFF, My mother has inadvertently sat on a bee, wasp or hornet.

Foreign students of our language are surprised to find that it contains words which are apparently of Japanese origin. A common greeting is —

HEHYU or HIYU

Other words borrowed from the Land of the Rising Sun are —

OBI JINGSAM WABBIT, I am exceedingly fatigued.

WANNA SUKAT, as in the hospitable invitation "Do you want a suck at my orange?"

GONNIGEISHASANG? Are you going to favour us with a ballad?

UCHAMSHI, I am somewhat diffident.

WHITWUNNA HREETHURTI? a request for racing information.

OMI WHITATUMMI, A comment made on observing a gentleman's pendulous stomach.

SAMURAI BUNGFU, A lady's rebuke to her bibulous husband, Sam.